SIMPLIFIED CONCEPTS ON E-BOOK PUBLISHING

MASTER GUIDE

MR INAH SYLVESTER

THIS BOOK IS DEDICATED TO GOD ALMIGHTY GOD

CONTENTS

BASIC EBOOK PUBLISHING

FIVE FUNDAMENTAL BENEFITS & GAINS FOR ATTENDING THIS FREE TRAINING ON THE BASIC METHOD OF PUBLISHING YOUR DREAM EBOOK

➢ You will be taught the basic method of eBook creation and publishing.

➢ You will be taught how to open your kdp account with Amazon at no cost.

➢ You will be taught how to publish your class/lecture notes using your kdp account.

➢ You will be taught how to write a strong and purposeful book. A bestseller

➢ You will learn how to go to kdp to publish your eBooks the basic way.

HOW CAN ONE BECOME A BEST SELLER ON AMAZON?

- ➢ By starting with a big idea
- ➢ Writing with the audience in mind
- ➢ Editing for clarity and not perfection
- ➢ Packaging my book with a global audience in mind
- ➢ Always promoting my book.

STRONG WRITING AND PURPOSEFUL WRITING

What is strong writing?

Writing a strong book goes beyond writing, it means writing a strong book in an actual sense of it. A strong writing, beyond meeting the literature, literary needs, should also meet the needs of your target audience, to an extent, they would be willing to pay for it or do anything to get your work. This definition makes up the best sellers.

Best sellers are not so called because they wrote well, but because they sell well. Writing is something else, but how well it is sold or sought afer is another ball game.

Strong writing may be writing in an appealing, inspring and acceptable manner. Strong writing must be contextual. The reason why someone like J.K ROBBINS, DANIELLE STEEL and other world acclaimed authors never lived the typical poor writer's life is because they understood strong writing and its purpose and benefits. Strong writing is contextual and problem-solving oriented. It is the effort to meet your audience need about a pressing subject.

Learning to stop writing when you feel like stopping is an important key to strong writing in order to avoid bad writing. This in most cases results to having so many voluminous books with poor content and no audience.

INTRODUCTION TO EBOOK PRODUCTION

"An electronic book, also known as an e-book or eBook, is a book publication made available in digital form, consisting of text, images, or both, readable on the flat-panel display of computers or other electronic devices". Also, an eBook is a non-editable, reflowable book that is converted to a digital format to be read on any digital device such as computer screens or mobile devices.

For starters, eBooks are files that you can read on a digital device – a tablet, smart phone, computer, etc. But again, considering other files can be read on digital devices (i.e. word documents) eBooks have specific characteristics that differentiate them. E-Books are better defined by their characteristics

EBOOKS SHOULDN'T BE EDITABLE

One distinct characteristic of an eBook: the text should not be editable. An eBook should always be converted into a format that ensures it's uneditable. With thousands of people having access to it on digital devices, people could potentially change any contpotentially change any content without the author's permission. So, in order to qualify as an actual eBook, text should not be able to be changed in any way, just like a paperback book. EBooks are eflowable (with an exception)

Another important characteristic is that true eBooks should be reflow able. This means that no matter what the size of the screen you're viewing the eBook on, it will always fit your screen; text will remain formatted with line breaks and chapters and images will resize to fit the proportions of the device you're reading on.

There is one exception though: PDFs. Considering PDFs can't be edited, but they aren't reflowable, they technically don't qualify as eBooks according to the characteristics that differentiate eBooks. But with businesses taking advantage of the ease of PDF downloads and distribution, PDFs have become "unofficial" eBooks and are still widely used eBook formats. There are several formats: eBook formats; EBUP, AZW, and PDF.

EPUB (.epub)

An EPUB, or electronic publication, is the most widely supported format.

A PDF, also known as a **portable document format,** isn't technically a true eBook according to our definition, but it's the format most people are familiar with. Amazon is well known for E-Book publication.

CREATING YOUR E-BOOK

Creating an eBook starts from the process of using Microsoft Word to format your document.

PREPARATION OF YOUR BOOK USING MICROSOFT WORD

Sections and Segments of your book to be converted to eBook or for normal publication. A book is expected to contain the following sections:

1. Cover page.
2. Copyright page.
3. Dedication, acknowledgement
4. Table of contents.
5. Introduction.
6. Body (or Chapters).
7. Back page (blurb/about the author).

This shall be discussed one after the other. However, note that the order above isn't sacrosanct.

You may alter the order from items 3 to 5. For you to have a good book, all these listed above must be there. Preparation and organization is a very important aspect of human activity, it is wrong to do things without adequate preparation and procedures, which in most cases produces error and dissatisfaction.

So let's pick them one after the other. Let's start with;

COVER PAGE

That's the first thing you see of a book

COPYRIGHT© PAGE

That's the protection ownership rights to the contents of the book.

Note of warning: the information written in any book in the copyright pages, tells you the extent to which you can use the contents and who to contact before usage.

Copyright abuse is a great crime. It can cost you money and your freedom- imprisonment.

This on a serious note and must not be toiled with. Times are changing, what you were able to get away with yesterday, one may not be so lucky today. **PLEASE NOTE.**

TABLE OF CONTENTS (TOC)

This is a quick guide for people to leap to a particular chapter. It comes with the chapter title and the page, dedication, acknowledgement, praise and/or foreword, are meant to boost reception and recognition of the book. Materials used besides others.

INTRODUCTION

This is meant to tell readers in summary what to expect from the book.

At what point do you think you should write your introduction? Writing your introduction before finishing your book interior contents may not convert and convey the right message. So rightly said by some persons, do that at the end. The best time to write your introduction, isn't before you create the interior, rather it comes after you have written the whole book.

BODY OR CHAPTERS OR INTERIOR

Here you start your story; this is where you write the content and what the book is about. The body of your book or chapters or interior.

Here is where you start your story. Whatever you wish to convey and the whole concept/gist. Here, remember all you have been thought about writing a strong book that sells. This is where you apply that knowledge that places you at the top and rewards you with the title of a Bestseller.

Last but not the least is;

ABOUT THE AUTHOR

This is a short description about you and should be written in the third person format.

INTRODUCTION TO FORMATTING

Practical Ways of Formatting your eBook using a customised template.

Formatting is the layout of your document in a presentable manner. It guides you in building your book in preparation for your eBook Creation and Publishing. Note that before your book can be accepted for publication on Amazon, there is a standard format that it must conform to.

Formatting your book is very critical to eBook publication in Amazon. We have manual method which involves the use of Microsoft tools. The digital method is very fast and error free. The digital method will be thoroughly taught at a Master class which will commence soon.

At least, we have 10 Practical Steps to Formatting. They are summarized as follows:

Step 1: Set your page and margin.

Step 2: Choose suitable styles and customise same.

Step 3: Format the interiors - chapters.

Step 4: Fix your cover designate

Step 5: Pagination

Step 6: Headers fixation

Step 7: Extras

Step 8: Add images if available - how?

Step 9: Table of contents (TOC)
Step 10: Proof and conversions to PDF.

You put your book to shape following the above steps manually. All the steps can be done on Microsoft word. Should you use some irregular sizes it may restrict your global book outreach on Amazon.
Note that: The most used and acceptable trim size is **6" x 9"**

This process of publishing eBooks means, you will get both digital publication and paperback publication at the end of the day.
On the layout tab, in the page setup, **click size, select paper,** then **paper size.** This opens a dialogue box.

TEMPLATE

T his is a physical object whose shape is used as a guide to make other objects.

A generic model or pattern from which other objects are based or derived.

I want all everyone to download the customized formatted MICROSOFT doc., which shall be sent shortly.

I want to unveil the Basic publishing solution.

The digital (kindle create app) to be taken at Masters class is amazing.

But before I share, I want to be sure we're ready for what is coming.

HOW TO USE CUSTOMIZED DOCS.

1. Edit what you see or delete
2. Replace it with what's in your manuscript.

HOW TO CREATE THE KDP ACCOUNT

Without a kdp account, there is a lot you cannot do on the amazing Amazon app.

This is a practical class and one of the requirements for graduation is that your

book(s) must be published using Kindle Create app (during your Master's Class). In the Masters class, among many other things, you will be taught;

HOW TO GET YOUR ISBN FREE OF CHARGE.

How to design your paperback yourself without spending, but for data.

How to style your book interior yourself.

How to upload your book to Amazon platform without spending a kobo, but for data.

How to publish for others using only your laptop and data, and many more.

This evening is the grand finale of the Basic training on eBook publication on Amazon. Remember, great opportunity often appears small.

Are you an academia? Those researches you spent time and money shouldn't just end in archive. They can be converted to lifetime revenue.

Are you a Pastor? Those sermons, bible teachings counseling and inspirational books can be made global:

Are you a civil servant? Your experience in your discipline can be converted to impart the world.

Are you a student? Short poems, stories and ideas will fetch you more than you can imagine.

E Book on Amazon avail you great opportunity to convert your potential to global resources. However, you will only get to gain all it requires in Master's class. Therefore, I will advise you to get set for the Master's class that will commence on the 3rd of April, 2021. Opening your kdp account is the core of the training. That is what you will be using for your eBook publication and to monitor your payment. In case you have challenge with your tax issue, this will be of help. From the tax information bar, click provide tax information or click answer tax interview.

Tax classification: **Select individual.**

For U.S. tax purpose, are you a U.S. person? **Select No**

Are you acting as intermediary? **Select No.**

Type your full name and country.

Unclick I have a non US Tin and select the first option I.e the country where I am liable...

Click continue.

Use your full name as your signature

Click Save and preview.

Then finally submit form.

YOU CANNOT AFFORD TO REMAIN ANALOGUE

The Stone Age ended not because there were no more stones.

That your forbearers did things certain ways doesn't mean you should continue on that path. There's a better way!

I love the Bible passage which states that ***"Remove not the old landmark which your parents have set."***

The first time I heard that, so great sense and sensibility were developed in me as a person.

THE MESSAGE

What this insinuations means is that "don't alter your parents good legacies," and it doesn't in anyway admonish us to continue to live in mud houses, in this era of sophisticated construction materials.